Primordial Strength Systems Pool Explosive Power Endurance Training One
By Steven Helmicki

All rights reserved. No part of this manual may be reproduced without author's written consent, except for briefs quotations in articles or reviews.

Copyright 2010 Primordial Strength Inc.
ISBN 978-0-557-29861-7

These are brief workouts that can be used as additional conditioning on your off days Or as entry level, short intense beginning workouts. Always be cautious. Maintain grip on implements, full concentration, maintained pool floor or safe, clean footing in a lake or other body of water is an absolute must. The trainee should always have a partner or lifeguard on duty while swimming or performing pool training. You must have completed at least intermediate primordial strength to proceed with additional workouts on off days. Follow workouts 101 through 129 and then repeat the cycle with greater velocity. A full trainee who is training the Monday, Wednesday, Friday template should perform these workouts on Tuesday and Thursday as active restoration.

Pool 101

Submerged to waist height 2kg kettlebell swings x 2 immediately followed by 4kg kettlebell swing x 2 repeat four times non-stop

Submerged to waist height 2kg kettlebell vertical jump x 1 immediately followed by 4kg kettlebell vertical jump x 1 repeat 3 times non-stop

3 minutes of free swim moderate pace.

Pool 102

Submerged to waist height 6kg kettlebell front squats x 2 immediately followed by 12kg kettlebell front squats x 2 repeat four times non-stop

Submerge to waist height 6kg kettlebell clean x 2 immediately followed by 12kg kettlebell clean x 2 repeat four times non-stop

2 minutes of full intensity swimming

Pool 103

Submerged to neck height 4kg kettlebell overhead press x 2 immediately followed by 8kg press x 2 repeat 6 times non-stop

Submerge to waist height 4kg kettlebell row x 3 immediately followed by 8kg x 3 repeat three times non-stop

4 minutes of slow swimming

Pool 104

Submerge to elbow height 4kg kettlebell curls x 3 reps 4 seconds rest x 2 reps 6 seconds rest 5 reps 4 seconds rest 1 rep 3 seconds rest 6 repeat until completely fatigued

7 minutes of intermediate paced swimming.

Pool 105

Submerge to waist height two bodyweight snatches immediately followed by 4kg kettlebell snatches x 2 immediately followed by 8kg kettlebell snatches x 2 repeat three times non-stop

3 minutes of full intensity swimming.

Pool 106

Submerge to waist height 4kg kettlebell cleans x 2 immediately followed by 8kg kettlebell cleans x 2 repeat 5 times non-stop

Submerge to chest height bodyweight vertical jumps x 2 reps 6 seconds rest x 5 sets

2 minutes slow swim.

Pool 107

Submerge to knee height and perform kneeling to standing jumps x 2 reps 5 seconds rest x 5 sets

10 minutes slow swim.

Pool 108

Submerge to waist height 8kg kettlebell deadlifts x 3 immediately followed by 16kg kettlebells x 3 repeat 5 times non-stop

4 minutes intermediate swim

Pool 109

Submerge to chest height and perform 8kg kettlebell vertical jumps x 1 rep 5 seconds rest x 8 sets

2 minutes high intensity swim

Pool 110

Submerge knee height kettlebell bent rows 4 kg x 2 immediately followed by 8kg x 2 immediately followed by 12kg x 2 repeat three times non-stop

3 minutes slow swim

Pool 111

Pool step squats bodyweight x 2 immediately followed by 4kg kettlebell x 2 immediately followed by 8kg kettlebell x 2 repeat 4 times non-stop

6 minute intermediate paced swim

Pool 112

Pool step step-ups bodyweight x 2 immediately followed by 4kg x 2 immediately followed by 8kg x 2 repeat 3 times non-stop

4 minutes high intensity swim

Pool 113

Swim flush 10 slow laps alternating crawl, breaststroke, backstroke, butterfly, free style

Pool 114

Submerge to chest height with 4 kg kettlebells perform all in a row- 15 knee ups, 15 calf raises, 15 overhead presses, 15 shrugs, 15 curls repeat twice.

2 minutes slow swim

Pool 115

Submerge to elbow height 2kg medicine ball triceps pushdowns x 3 immediately followed by 4 kg medicine ball triceps pushdowns x 3 repeat 4 times non-stop

3 minute intermediate swim

Pool 116

Submerge to chest height double mini band assisted rows 3 reps x 6 sets 5 seconds rest

4 minutes high intensity swimming

Pool 117

Free style short swim sprint 10 yards immediately followed by 10 yards slow repeat 10 times non-stop

Pool 118

Submerge to chest height slow jog in place x 8 seconds immediately followed by 5 second sprint in place repeat 12 times non-stop

3 minute slow swim

Pool 119

Submerge to chest height vertical jump x 1 immediately followed by sprint in place x 4 seconds repeat 6 times non-stop

3 minute intermediate swim

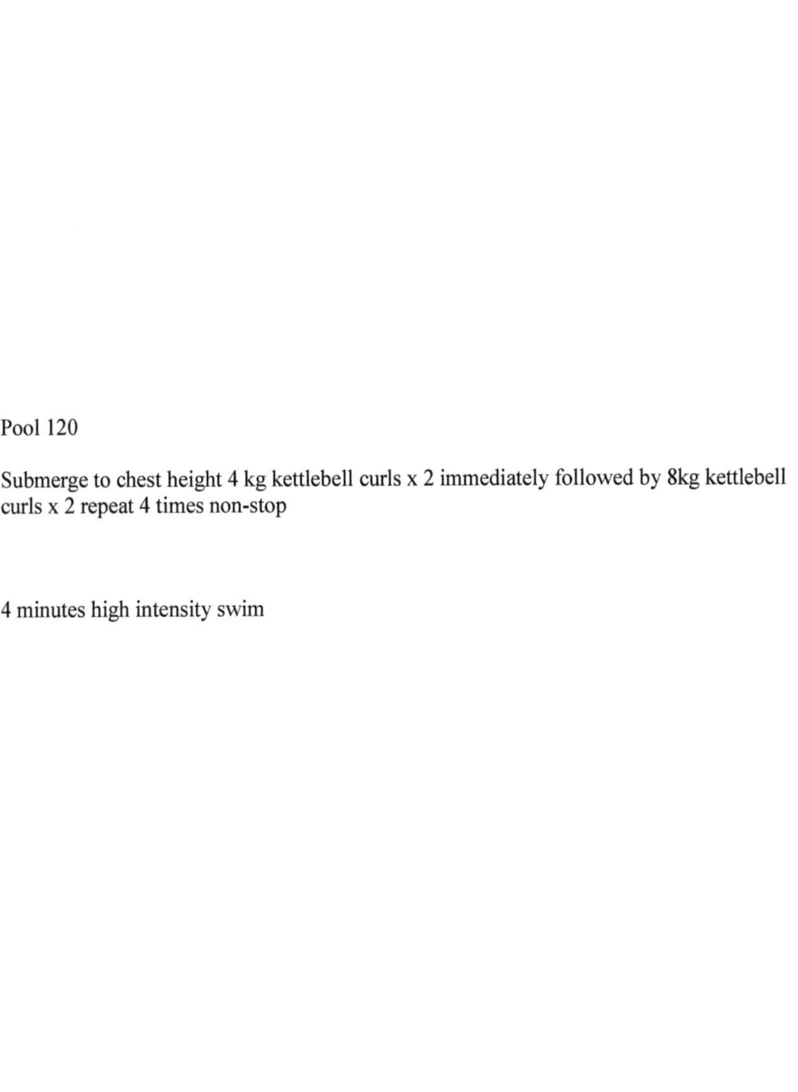

Pool 120

Submerge to chest height 4 kg kettlebell curls x 2 immediately followed by 8kg kettlebell curls x 2 repeat 4 times non-stop

4 minutes high intensity swim

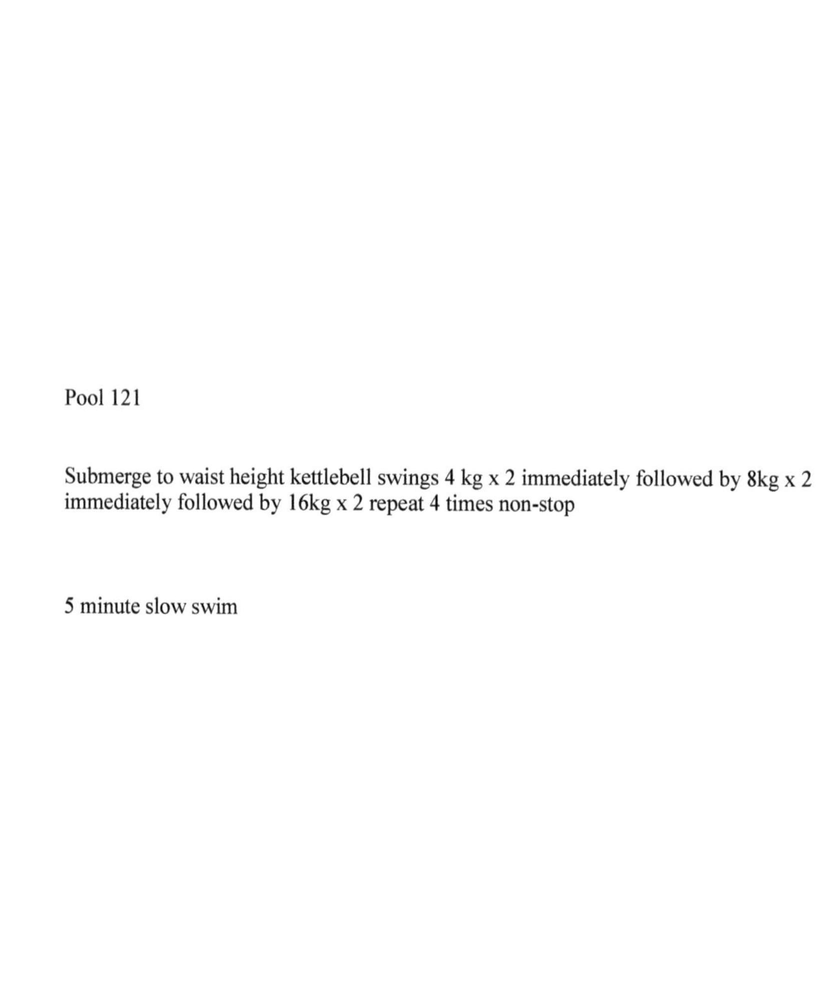

Pool 121

Submerge to waist height kettlebell swings 4 kg x 2 immediately followed by 8kg x 2 immediately followed by 16kg x 2 repeat 4 times non-stop

5 minute slow swim

Pool 122

Submerge to waist height kettlebell bent over rows 4kg x 2 immediately followed by 8kg x 2 immediately followed by 16kg x 2 repeat 3 times non-stop

2.5 minutes high intensity swim

Pool 123

10 minute straight swim at medium pace alternating stroke pattern

Pool 124

Submerge to waist height 4kg kettlebell front jump squats x 2 reps x 3 sets 5 seconds rest

20 yard swim sprints x 13 sets with 10 seconds rest

Pool 125

Submerge to elbow height 4kg kettlebell front jump squats x 2 reps x 2 sets 5 seconds rest

10 yard swim sprints x 10 sets with 5 seconds rest

Pool 126

Submerge to chest height 4kg kettlebell upright rows x 3 immediately followed by 8kg kettlebell upright rows x 3 repeat 3 times non-stop

5 minute slow swim

Pool 127

Submerge to waist height 6kg kettlebell high pull x 2 immediately followed by 12kg kettlebell high pull x 2 repeat 3 times non-stop

8 minute intermediate swim

Pool 128

Submerge to waist height light band attached to waist two step sprint starts x 4 times 4 seconds rest

2 minute high intensity swim.

Pool 129

Submerge to waist height light band attached to waist two step sprint start x 2 immediately followed by average band two step sprint start x 2 repeat 3 times non-stop

30 seconds high intensity swim rest 30 seconds repeat 5 times

www.ingramcontent.com/pod-product-compliance
Ingram Content Group UK Ltd.
Pitfield, Milton Keynes, MK11 3LW, UK
UKHW041902190726
13854UKWH00003B/1032